The Joy of Sisters

&

by Karen Brown

Meadowbrook Press

Distributed by Simon & Schuster
New York

Library of Congress Cataloging-in-Publication Data

Brown, Karen
  The joy of sisters / by Karen Brown.
  p   ;   cm.
  ISBN 0-88166-295-X
  1. Sisters—Quotations, maxims, etc. I. Title.
PN6084.S56B76   1997
818'.5402—dc21   97-16066
                                        CIP

Simon & Schuster Ordering # 0-671-57681-X
Meadowbrook ISBN # 0-88166-295-X

Editor: Bruce Lansky
Editorial Coordinators: Michael Platzer and Steven Roe
Production Manager: Joe Gagne
Production Assistant: Danielle White
Photo Editor: Maggie Merkow
Cover Designer: Danielle White
Cover Photography (clockwise from left): © 1995 by Bill Lai. Used by permission of Photo
Bank, Inc.; © 1997 by SuperStock; © 1997 by P. Beck/Frozen Images; © 1997 by
SuperStock; © by Jim Whitmer; © by Jim Whitmer

Published by Meadowbrook Press, 5451 Smetana Drive, Minnetonka, MN 55343

BOOK TRADE DISTRIBUTION by Simon & Schuster, a division of Simon and Schuster,
Inc., 1230 Avenue of the Americas, New York, NY 10020

01 00 99 98   10 9 8 7 6 5 4 3 2

Printed in the United States of America

Acknowledgments

We would like to thank the individuals who served on a reading panel for this project: Teresa Bateman, Margaret Park Bridges, Dorothy Brummel, Gail H. Clark, Faye Click, Tamera L. Collins, Olga Cossi, Holly Davis, Rebecca Dotlich, Nancy Flood, Ruthie Hawkinson, Laura Irvin, Sydnie Kleinhenz, Wendy Lees, Jean H. Marvin, Janet McCann, Ingrid McCleary, Barbara Merchant, Jeanne M. Nelson, Elaine Nick, Josephine "Joi" Nobisso, Elizabeth Paterra, Renee Paulson, C. S. Pederson, Reggie Platzer, Lori Reed, Joan Marie Saxon, Mildred Schantz, Rosemary J. Schmidt, Mary Scott, Irene Sedeora, Esther Towns, Evelyn A. Wade, Maryan Winsor, and Vicki Wiita.

We would also like to thank the photographers who contributed to this book: pp. 3, 10, 40, and 86 © 1997 by SuperStock; p. 15 © by Randy M. Ury/The Stock Market Photo Agency; p. 20 © 1997 by P. Beck/Frozen Images; pp. 25 and 65 © 1989 and 1995 (respectively) by Bill Lai. Used by permission of Photo Bank, Inc.; pp. 28, 33, 56, 74, and 81 © by Jim Whitmer; p. 47 © 1996 by Harry Cutting; and p. 93 © 1993 by RB Studio. Used by permission of The Stock Market Photo Agency.

Introduction

Those of us with sisters know how lucky we are to experience this special lifetime relationship. From the secrets of childhood through the pangs of adolescence and on to the challenges of adult life, we know that we can count on a sister to share everything, to laugh and cry with us, to lend an ear or a helping hand, and most of all, to be a cherished and loyal friend.

The Joy of Sisters is a tribute to sisters everywhere, and I hope that in these pages you find something that will serve as a remembrance of your most treasured sentiments of sisterhood.

Karen Brown

Sisterhood is like electricity. It's an
invisible but powerful connection.

With sisters, the only strings attached
are from the heart.

The invisible ties between sisters
are often the strongest bonds.

Sisters together are a force
to be reckoned with.

You and your sister.
It's a win/win situation.

Selfless
Inspirational
Supportive
Trusting
Encouraging
Reliable
SISTERS

Your sister is God's gift to you.

When you have two sisters
you're twice-blessed.

Sisterhood is a celebration of life,
love, and family.

You don't get something for nothing,
except your sister's loyalty.

Your sister gives from the heart
and expects nothing in return.

Sisterhood is made up of small sacrifices—
and large rewards.

Sisters know that their relationship is based on give-and-take, and that sometimes one sister has to give more than her share.

Sisters know that the effort required in a relationship is like peeling an onion—it's a lot of work, and it can make you cry.

Nothing is so wondrous as the birth
of your much-longed-for child—
or the birth of your sister's.

No one finds your children as charming
and brilliant as you do—except your sister!

Sisters earn their place in heaven when
they take care of each other's kids.

For sisters, seeing their children carry on family traditions gives hope for the future.

As sisters watch their children at play, they realize that the more things change, the more they stay the same.

Who says you can't go home again?
Wherever you and your sister are,
there it is!

Your sister knows that the most important
furnishing in a home is love.

Sisters are often the glue that holds
families together.

She walks on the wild side;
you, on the straight-and-narrow.
But when it comes to family,
you always meet in the middle.

Charity does begin at home. You can ask
your sister for favors that you'd never ask
of anyone else!

Blood is thicker than water, and you can
count on your sister when you need
a transfusion of confidence.

Older sisters offer footsteps to follow when the path seems confusing.

Younger sisters are grateful to older ones for paving the way for such important milestones as dating, curfews, and makeup.

As you travel the road of life, your sister can give you directions.

A smart sister knows that example
is much more powerful than advice.

Imitation is the sincerest form of flattery,
especially when a younger sister
emulates an older one.

Your sister believes you are wise,
especially when you come to her
for advice!

A wise sister tells you to always put off until
tomorrow what you shouldn't do at all!

A sister will tell you that it's important to
know how the wind blows, especially when
you forget to wear a slip.

Your sister can help you see that some mistakes are lessons, not tragedies.

❦

Your sister reminds you that a mistake is proof that you tried.

❦

A wise sister helps you grow better, and not bitter, when faced with disappointments.

A wise sister will encourage you to
keep trying in trying times.

When you're worried about what you *can't*
do, your sister points out what you *can* do.

When you feel like a wannabe, your sister
assures you that you already *are*.

Two's company,
especially between sisters.

Busy sisters *always* make time
for each other.

No matter how busy you are,
your sister always comes first.

Between sisters, familiarity breeds contentment.

Sisterhood is the comfort of a "we" instead of the loneliness of an "I."

An evening with your sister and a bag of popcorn produces food for thought— and for the soul.

One of the best home remedies for loneliness is a visit from your sister.

Your sister is always happy to see you— even if you've stopped by unannounced, and her house is a mess.

Smart sisters know when to visit, and when to keep their distance.

With a sister, no matter how old you are
you can still lapse into childish behavior.

Sometimes you and your sister are
children disguised as grownups—
giggling and whispering to see what
you can get away with.

When you're with your sister, you don't
have to act your age.

Sisters are never too old to giggle
like children.

&

Sisters' laughter can turn into tears at jokes
no one else would understand.

&

Smart sisters know that a good day is not
complete without laughter.

Sisters can have a rollicking good time together doing absolutely nothing.

Sisters know that early to bed and early to rise means that they'll miss all the fun.

Sisters know that to be totally sane, they have to have moments of craziness.

Sisters know that anything worth having
is worth a shopping trip!

Your sister's closet has always been your
favorite place to shop—and, of course,
the price is right!

Your sister knows when it's your turn to be
on stage—and it's her turn to lead
the applause.

When you're on a winning streak,
your sister will be the first to greet you
at the finish line with a blue ribbon.

Your sister always wants the best
for you—and helps you do
whatever it takes to get it.

Your sister's words of encouragement are
often the boost you need to accomplish
your goal.

Your sister takes pleasure in your
accomplishments as if they were her own.

Your sister brings out the best in you—
and you in her.

Behind every great sister is another
who cheered her on.

Helping your sister row to a far-off shore
gets you there too.

૪

Your sister points out the beautiful scenery
as you travel the road to success.

૪

Your sister will help you reach for the stars
to find a little piece of heaven.

Sisters know the importance of following their hearts—and doing what they love.

Smart sisters know that life's greatest risks also yield its best rewards.

You know that your sister will always go the extra mile with you, even on an unpaved road.

Your sister is there when you need someone to lean on.

A wise sister knows when to lead, when to follow, and most importantly, when to walk by your side.

A sister's love can help lighten your load.

When your ship comes in,
your sister helps you unload it.

When there's work to be done,
your sister rolls up her sleeves.

When *you've* got a big problem, your sister
says, "What are *we* going to do?"

Your sister knows that two heads are better
than one—even if hers is barely above
water, and yours isn't screwed on right.

You can count on your sister to walk in
when everyone else has walked out.

When you're beginning to have doubts
about yourself, you can count on
your sister to believe in you.

When you're paralyzed by fear, your sister
gives you the self-confidence to take action.

Sisterhood is a lifelong conversation.

Conversations between sisters are like
a book that you can pick up at any time
and continue with ease.

With sisters' conversations, the well
never runs dry.

The most important rule of sisterhood is
to listen to each other.

The best thing about deep conversations
with your sister is that she really listens.

A sister's greatest gift to you
is her willingness to listen,
no matter how late the hour.

When your sister says, "Can we talk?" what
she really means is, "You talk. I'll listen."

A wise sister always tries to see things
from your point of view.

Your sister understands the words
that you don't say.

There are things you just don't have to
explain to your sister.

Blessed is the sister who knows when to
speak—and when to remain silent.

Sisters understand the silent language
of a warm embrace.

Between sisters, a silent touch
speaks volumes.

Your sister can make a statement without
saying a word by just raising her eyebrows.

As children, you hid your diary from your sister. Now, you *want* to tell her everything!

As children, you dreamed of a room of your own. Now, you can't wait to share a room with your sister—and stay up all night, talking.

You used to tell *on* your sister. Now you *tell* her everything.

The most precious gift sisters can give to
each other is themselves.

Sisters know that good news is better
when you share it with each other.

With your sister, you can think out loud.

With a sister as your confidante,
you can be confident.

Like your hairdresser and your shrink,
you can count on a sister to keep your
deepest, darkest secrets.

Sisters know that a long talk on the
front-porch swing will always take
precedent over piles of laundry.

Quality time: you and your sister
confiding in each other
while washing dishes.

When you're between a rock and a hard place, call your sister!

⚘

Your sister will discuss your latest dilemma with you—at 2:00 in the morning!

⚘

Your sister is someone who will indulge you when you need to rehash a gripe for the third time.

Talk, talk, talk.
Talk is cheap, except when your sister
moves to another coast.

&

When it comes to fitting conversations into
a long day, sisters have developed talking
on the phone—while fixing dinner and
changing the baby—into an art form.

Your sister shares your tears
and your triumphs.

&

Sisters' shared life is like a seesaw.
When you're down, she's up for you.
And you take turns.

&

Sisters are grateful for having each other
to share life's storms and to enjoy
the calm that follows.

Your sister knows when you need to laugh,
to keep from crying.

Sisters know that sometimes the best
solutions to big problems are reached with
the help of cookies, chips, and ice cream.

When you're a sister, you sympathize,
console, and commiserate—that's your job!

Sisters know that a helping hand
is just a hug away.

Your sister knows when you need flattery,
encouragement, and a big hug.

When a sister is guilty of loving too much,
it's a crime of the heart.

When you want to run away from home, your sister's house is a good place to go.

You can take off your hat on a bad
hair day when you're with your sister.

When you've had a bad perm, your sister
brings you her scarf collection.

Sisters sympathize when you have a good
hair day—and nowhere to go!

Your sister convinces you that there's a beautiful swan in the mirror, when all you can see is a silly goose.

A sister's like a makeover artist—she brings out the beauty in you.

Your sister has 20/20 vision, except where your faults are concerned.

When you're on a diet, your sister
orders salad too.

Your sister offers to wash and let you dry
when she knows you've just had
a $25.00 manicure.

When you're busily feathering your nest,
your sister donates her ostrich boa.

Sisters are like your favorite slippers—
warm, comfortable, and cozy.

When you've got cold feet, your sister's
support feels like warm slippers.

When fishing for compliments, you can
count on your sister to throw you a line.

Having your sister just a phone call away is like having your own private therapist.

Meeting your sisters after work for a drink used to be called happy hour. Now it's more like group therapy.

Your thoughtful sister sends you
Valentine's Day roses when you don't
have a boyfriend.

Your sister gives you her umbrella during
a storm, then helps you see the rainbow
afterward.

Sisters know that when you sow seeds of thoughtfulness, goodwill begins to grow.

Sisterhood is like a choir: you may sing different parts, but still produce beautiful harmony.

Sisters may march to different drummers, but they can still dance to the same beat.

Your sister respects you for being yourself.

Supportive sisters appreciate their
differences as much as their similarities.

Sisters know the importance of being true
to themselves—and to each other.

Your sister knows everything about you—
and loves you anyway.

Wise sisters know what to notice in each
other, and what to overlook.

A considerate sister doesn't insist
that you see everything through her eyes,
but allows you to use your own.

You and your sister may have had a
difference or two—but never
an indifference!

Grown-up sisters have learned to disagree
without being disagreeable.

A wise sister honors your opinion—
even when she doesn't agree.

A gracious sister will meet you halfway—
even if she thinks you're half-baked.

Your sister is brilliant and sensitive when
she sees your point, and just a little
misguided when she doesn't.

Your sister can't really prevent you from
doing anything wrong. But she can keep
you from enjoying it.

A sister's forgiveness is a welcome gift.

A savvy sis knows that the one who apologizes always gets the last word.

Your sister will be quick to forgive your faults—especially if you reciprocate.

When you get too puffed up, your sister
will poke you and let some air out.

A wise sister helps you see that if you're all
wrapped up in yourself, it's not a pretty
package!

When you're caught up in a flight of fancy,
your sister's words can bring you
back down to earth.

When you need to read between the lines, your sister hands you reading glasses.

It sometimes takes a savvy sister to help you separate fact from fiction.

When you're making mountains out of molehills, your sister will knock them down to size.

When charmed by a face across a crowded room, your sister reminds you that you can't see without your glasses.

Your sister will remind you of your rights
and your wrongs.

A supportive sister helps you find
the virtues in yourself, rather than
the vices in others.

Your sister gives you the kind of advice
you *need* to hear—not just what
you *want* to hear.

A sensitive sister offers criticisms in private
and compliments in public.

Your sister may be aware of your faults
but would never admit them to
anyone else.

You can count on your sister to talk about
you behind your back—and say
good things.

Sometimes the light at the end of the
tunnel is your sister with a flashlight.

A sister's love is like a candle that lights up
the dark places in your life.

When you're about to burn a bridge,
your practical sister makes you
cross it first.

When you're tripping down a dangerous
path, your sister pulls you up
to the high road.

You need a sister to help you out of the difficult trouble that was so easy for you to get into all alone!

When your life is in need of repairs, your sister arrives with her tool kit.

Your sister helps you pick up the pieces and mend a situation you thought beyond repair.

Your sister never gets in your way, unless you're on the way down.

When you're finally at the end of your rope, your sister helps you tie a knot so you can keep hanging on.

Your sister's concern helps soften the blows when you've learned a lesson from the school of hard knocks.

Sisterhood includes sharing a burden that becomes too heavy for one.

Between sisters, love may not conquer all—but it can certainly ease the pain.

Between sisters, stories of your childhood
never get boring—they just get better
and better!

Being with your sister enables you
to travel backward in time.

Home movies, dusty scrapbooks, and a
closet full of memories—sisters can turn
back the hands of time!

Reminiscing with your sister is like refinishing a fine antique: you carefully strip away layers of memories and chip away at family myths to get to the core of things.

Sisters know the fun of taking the skeletons out of the closet—and making them dance a little.

Between sisters, a rediscovered memory can cause goose bumps.

Sisters reminiscing: so many subjects,
so little time.

Loving sisters understand the joy
of a shared memory.

For sisters, the past is full of
Kodak moments.

Sisters always stick together through thick and thin—and dieting in-between.

Sisters know that you can grow old gracefully—or wear a very large muumuu.

A little white lie is okay when your sister asks if her legs are beginning to look like Great Aunt Bertha's.

Sisters often look at each other as if
in a mirror—with shared experiences
etched on their faces.

Sisters know that wrinkles are just life's
"Certificate of Achievement" for laughter—
and tears.

Your sister's remembrances are cherished,
but so is her ability to forget.

Sisters enjoy laughing together over
experiences that were once painful.

Sisters who grow old together realize that
all happiness has been obtained with some
degree of pain.

You and your sister used to know all the answers. Now you realize that sometimes you don't even know the questions.

Your sister said that one day you'd appreciate her—and now you finally do!

Sisterhood is a club with a lifetime membership.

Everyone should be their own best friend—
but it never hurts to have a sister
as a backup!

Diamonds are nice, but a *sister* is a girl's
best friend.

Your sister is there for you—
today and always.

Sisters know that, no matter what,
they will always have each other.

A sister will do anything for you—
any time, any place, any way.

Out of sight, out of mind? Not with sisters!

No matter how far away you live,
you and your sisters are always close.

Friends drift apart, pets come and go,
and neighbors move away, but the bonds
of sisterhood endure forever.

The Joy of Friendship
by Robert Scotellaro

This collection of wit and wisdom is the perfect gift to share with a friend. Sometimes sentimental, sometimes humorous, but always right on, *The Joy of Friendship* will bring the best of friends to an even better understanding of what friendship is all about. Illustrated with 15 black-and-white photos that poignantly depict friendship.

Order #3506

The Joy of Marriage
by Monica and Bill Dodds

Here's a book of romance and love for married couples. With clever one-line messages, it accentuates the everyday romantic, caring, and playful elements of married life:

- A marriage license is really just a learner's permit.
- Love is letting your spouse have the last piece of pie.
- The great thing about being married a long time is falling in love with the same person again...and again...and again.

Filled with beautiful, touching black-and-white photographs, it's the perfect gift for weddings and anniversaries.

Order #3504

The Joy of Parenthood
by Jan Blaustone

This book contains hundreds of warm and inspirational "nuggets" of wisdom to help prepare parents for the pleasures and challenges ahead. Twenty-four touching black-and-white photos help convey the joy of parenthood and make this a delightful book to give or receive.

Order #3500

The Joy of Grandparenting
by Audrey Sherins
and Joan Holleman

This book will have grandparents smiling in agreement as they read these modern proverbs. It contains wit and wisdom on such issues as grandparents as role models; passing on family heritage; the uniqueness of each grandchild; the role of grandparent, parent, and child; showing off grandchildren; and the future. Audrey Sherins describes being a grandparent as "all the pleasure and none of the responsibility of parenthood."

Order #3502

Order Form

Qty.	Title	Author	Order No.	Unit Cost (U.S. $)	Total
	Age Happens	Lansky, B.	4025	$7.00	
	Are You Over the Hill?	Dodds, B.	4265	$6.00	
	Dads Say the Dumbest Things!	Lansky/Jones	4220	$6.00	
	Familiarity Breeds Children	Lansky, B.	4015	$7.00	
	For Better And For Worse	Lansky, B.	4000	$7.00	
	Golf: It's Just a Game!	Lansky, B.	4035	$7.00	
	Grandma Knows Best	McBride, M.	4009	$7.00	
	How to Line Up Your Fourth Putt	Rusher, B.	4075	$7.00	
	Joy of Friendship	Scotellaro, R.	3506	$7.00	
	Joy of Grandparenting	Sherins/Holleman	3502	$7.00	
	Joy of Marriage	Dodds, M. & B.	3504	$7.00	
	Joy of Parenthood	Blaustone, J.	3500	$7.00	
	Joy of Sisters	Brown, K.	3508	$7.00	
	Lovesick	Lansky, B.	4045	$7.00	
	Moms Say the Funniest Things!	Lansky, B.	4280	$6.00	
				Subtotal	
				Shipping and Handling (see below)	
				MN residents add 6.5% sales tax	
				Total	

YES! Please send me the books indicated above. Add $2.00 shipping and handling for the first book and 50¢ for each additional book. Add $2.50 to total for books shipped to Canada. Overseas postage will be billed. Allow up to four weeks for delivery. Send check or money order payable to Meadowbrook Press. No cash or COD's, please. Prices subject to change without notice. Quantity discounts available upon request.

Send book(s) to:

Name _____ Address _____

City _____ State ____ Zip _____ Telephone (_____) _____

P.O. number (if necessary) _____

Payment via: ❏ Check or money order payable to Meadowbrook Press   Amount enclosed $_____

❏ Visa ❏ MasterCard (for orders over $10.00 only)

Account # _____ Signature _____ Exp. Date _____

A FREE Meadowbrook Press catalog is available upon request.

Mail to: Meadowbrook Press.
5451 Smetana Drive, Minnetonka, MN 55343
Phone (612) 930-1100   Toll-Free (800) 338-2232   Fax (612) 930-1940